GW00498916

To

From

Published in 2011 by Helen Exley Giftbooks in Great Britain.
Illustrations by Caroline Gardner © Caroline Gardner Publishing 2009.
All illustrations based on the Caroline Gardner Elfin, Bloom and Everso rang
All words by Pam Brown © Helen Exley Creative Ltd 2011.
Text, selection and arrangement © Helen Exley Creative Ltd 2011.
The moral right of the author has been asserted.

12 11 10 9 8 7 6 5 4 3 2

ISBN: 978-1-84634-544-9

Edited by Helen Exley.

Printed in China.

Helen Exley Giftbooks, 16 Chalk Hill, Watford,
Herts, WD19 4BG, UK.
www.helenexleygiftbooks.com

To my great Friend

WORDS BY PAM BROWN
ILLUSTRATIONS BY CAROLINE GARDNER

A HELEN EXLEY GIFTBOOK

A real friend

A friend gives time and care
and affection...
Forgives your foibles,
sees your virtues,
rejoices in your triumphs,
comforts you in sorrow.
A friend makes giving a joy
and sharing a delight.

Our friendships
make us more than
we are

On a sudden
summer's day

A friend calls you up
on a sudden summer's day
and says "Drop everything…
we're going out into the country
and finding ourselves lunch."

Friendship teaches us not only how to give - but how to take, with love and gratitude

Kindness

A friend values
above all else the words
"You were always kind to me."

A friend is the one who,
on the busiest day,
can find a scrap of time for a smile
and a cheerful word.

A friend gives you
more than your fair share
of her umbrella.

You

Nothing is so much fun without you to turn to and exclaim "Oh, look!" or "How on earth...?" Without that sharing, things lose their meaning. I need your laughter, your astonishment, your sympathy, your understanding.

A friend praises you behind your back

A real friend goes on being your friend when you're just about unspeakable.

A good friend, seeing you sink deeper and deeper into some appalling misjudgement, warns you – but accepts your decision. And stands by with a lifebelt.

Surprises!

*T*hank you for the stupendous,
the outrageous surprises
that light up the dull days.

*T*he potted plant
on your doorstep with no message
is from your friend.

*T*hank you for the many,
many times you've knocked
and said,
"I saw this and I thought of you."

*O*nly a true friend brings you
an enormous red balloon
in hospital.

There's no nee

A friend knows when
to talk things through, but,
most of all, a friend knows
when to keep absolutely quiet.
And to put the kettle on.

Friends can
enjoy talk- but
share silence.

o speak ...

*F*riendship can be
keeping silence.

*H*ere is a gift.
A night of gentle rain.
The scent of grass.
A pattering
against the window–pane.
A sighing of soft air shifting
the spangled leaves.
A time to share in silence.

Loyalty...

A fairly good friend will tell you not to worry and that it will all come right.

A perfect friend helps you face the truth and stays beside you, whatever comes.

A friend can know you
are disorganized and incompetent
with anything mechanical.
She can know you are inclined
to eat far too much chocolate.
And yet she still stays
your friend. And stands by
to pick up the pieces.

A friend
is a person
with whom
you dare to be
yourself

A friend finds a way
of telling you something
you've done is no good,
but making you feel it
was a good trial run for
something far, far better.

When you really need a friend

Friends are on permanent
stand-by to pick up the pieces
in disasters – big or little.

There are times when
we most need friends.
Ready to do anything
or go anywhere.
Thank you for doing,
being, just that.

*O*nly a real friend will accompany
you to the hospital
or the dentist – and wait.

A friend comes with you
when you demand to see
the manager. And manages,
without saying a word,
to look like a solicitor.

A friend comes round
when you are in despair
and does not try to jolly you
out of it.

Always thoughtful

A friend saves newspaper cuttings to amuse you, books for you to borrow, a frozen piece of pie, jumble sale discoveries, postcards, apples, foreign stamps and seedlings.

A root from your most beautiful penstemon. A recipe.
A cutting from a magazine.
A question.
"I haven't heard from you.
Are you OK?"
A warmth to keep the heart alive.

Strength

The sad thing about human beings
is that they never believe that bad
things can happen to them – only to
other people. It is our friends who
help us through our disillusions.

A look of sympathy,
of encouragement;
a hand reached out in kindness.
And all else is secondary.

A friend takes all your miseries
and reshapes them into hope.

*F*riends are people who go on conspiratorial shopping sprees together, diving in and out of shops totally beyond their price range, and ending up eating oozing cream cakes with only just enough money to get home.

*F*riend: with you around, the world can never be a lonely place.
Your step on the path, your knock at the door, your smile–
and the day is brighter.
A little pleasure – but one I treasure – putting a red ring round a calendar date to show I'll see you soon.

Life would be
full of dull patches
- if it wasn't
for friends

One specia...

Most friendships grow slowly,
over many years – but ours
seemed to come complete.
Sometimes I feel we've
known each other long before
we met. I was just waiting for you
to arrive in person.

riend

*O*n a most ordinary day
something wonderful can happen.
Out of the commonplace may come
the sight of something remarkable.
An astonishment.
A friend.
These are no ordinary days.

Across the miles

A friend can live in the next house the next street, the next town, the next country... or across an ocean. Friendship does not blur with distance. A friend is always present in heart and mind.

Friends are friends even when distance divides – for they think of each other, save jokes and curiosities to share, try to hold fast to marvels seen or heard to parcel as a gift.

The little smile
in passing,
the daft surprise
- these are what
endure and make
my life a joy.

It is the small, insignificant,
simple gestures that make life
bearable. A smile, a touch,
a word, a kindness, a concern.

*F*riendship can be a postcard,
a phone call,
a bunch of flowers,
a word of thanks,
a cup of tea,
a lift in the car,
a trip to the chemist.
A listening ear.

*I*t is the net
of small kindnesses
that holds humanity
together.

A friend believes in you

You have been there for me,
always; loving me when I was
near impossible to love.
Advising when I could be persuaded
to listen. Helping me, even when
I did not deserve your help.
Believing in me when anyone else
would have walked away.

A friend believes in you when
no one else does – and that
includes yourself,
listens when she's heard the tale
before – a hundred times,
is there for you when things
go wrong – and never says
I told you so, helps you
pick up the pieces
– and glues the bits together.

The whole world over, friends escap
the monotonies, the drudgeries, of
everyday existence – along well-
trodden tracks, laughing together at
the river's edge or in the market
square, exchanging ribaldries from
balconies, resting for a moment from

the blinding sun or driving rain.
A net of companionship encircling
the planet. Strength regained.
Sympathies exchanged. Bitterness
turned to warmth. Life made
endurable in shared experience,
in laughter and in courage.

Two lives

Girl friends move through the years
together – both of us equally
astounded at the things that life has
arranged for us. Things we did not
foresee, did not suspect. We talk over
coffee tables, in gardens, on
windswept esplanades and wonder at
the marvels and the miseries we have
encountered. Those who have not
known us, take our ways for granted –
but we both live in amazement at
each other's survival.

A lifelong friend

A friend can recognise you
after a gap of forty years.
The girl you walked home with
is going to meet you
for coffee and cakes one day,
when you are both white-haired
grandmothers, and you'll think
that neither of you has
aged one bit.

Shared memories

*I*t's the little incidents that bind
two friends together
– the remembrance of small,
silly things that will outlast
the days of youth.

*O*ur lives are interlocked.
Your happiness, your sorrow,
are mine.
And mine, yours.

One sheds so many friendships
with the passing years –
lost to distance and to
circumstance.
But you have been there,
part of my life,
part of my memories.
And will be, I hope, forever.

Our triumphs rust a little
with the years.
But our friendship is golden and
shines as bright as new.

One good friend
lasts a lifetime

Wishes for you

*M*ay the future bring every
happiness, the fulfilment
of your dreams, many friends
and lasting love.

*M*ay the coming years bring you
new hopes, new beginnings,
new adventures, new discoveries.

*M*ay I always be here for you.

Thank you

Thank you for
all you have given me.
Your laughter,
your patience,
your kindness,
your friendship.

Thank you for being
who you are.
Unique. Wonderful.
My friend.

Helen Exley runs her own publishing company, which sells giftbooks in more than seventy countries. Helen's books cover the many events and emotions in life. Caroline Gardner's delightfully quirky and bright illustrations paired with Pam Brown's insightful and beautiful words create this stunning new range.

Caroline Gardner Publishing has been producing beautifully designed stationery from offices overlooking the River Thames in England since 1993 and has been developing the distinctive new ranges for many years.

WHAT IS A HELEN EXLEY GIFTBOOK?

Helen Exley Giftbooks cover the most powerful
range of all human relationships:
love between couples, the bonds with families
and between friends. No expense is spared in making
sure that each book is as thoughtful and meaningful
a gift as it is possible to create:
good to give, good to receive. You have the result in
your hands. If you have loved it — tell others!
There is no power like
word-of-mouth recommendation.

For a complete listing of all titles and gifts, visit:
www.helenexleygiftbooks.com

Helen Exley Giftbooks
16 Chalk Hill,
Watford, Herts,
WD19 4BG, UK.
www.helenexleygiftbooks.com